# ANIMALS
### That Make a Difference!

# Ants

**Ashley Lee**

Explore other books at:
WWW.ENGAGEBOOKS.COM

VANCOUVER, B.C.

℮ WWW.ENGAGEBOOKS.COM

*Ants: Level 2*
*Animals That Make a Difference!*
Lee, Ashley 1995 –
Text © 2020 Engage Books
Design © 2020 Engage Books

Edited by: A.R. Roumanis and
Lauren Dick

Text set in Arial Regular.
Chapter headings set in Arial Black.

FIRST EDITION / FIRST PRINTING

LIBRARY AND ARCHIVES CANADA CATALOGUING IN PUBLICATION

Title: Ants: Animals That Make a Difference Level 2 reader / Ashley Lee
Names: Lee, Ashley, 1995- author

Identifiers: Canadiana (print) 20200308963 | Canadiana (ebook) 20200308971
ISBN 978-1-77437-621-8 (hardcover)
ISBN 978-1-77437-622-5 (softcover)
ISBN 978-1-77437-623-2 (pdf)
ISBN 978-1-77437-624-9 (epub)
ISBN 978-1-77437-625-6 (kindle)

Subjects:
LCSH: Ants—Juvenile literature
LCSH: Human-animal relationships—Juvenile literature

Classification: LCC QL568.F7 L44 2020 | DCC J595.79/6—DC23

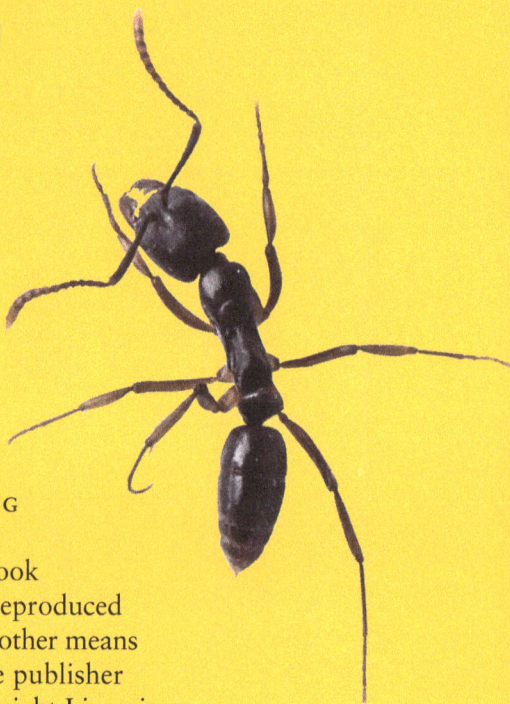

# Contents

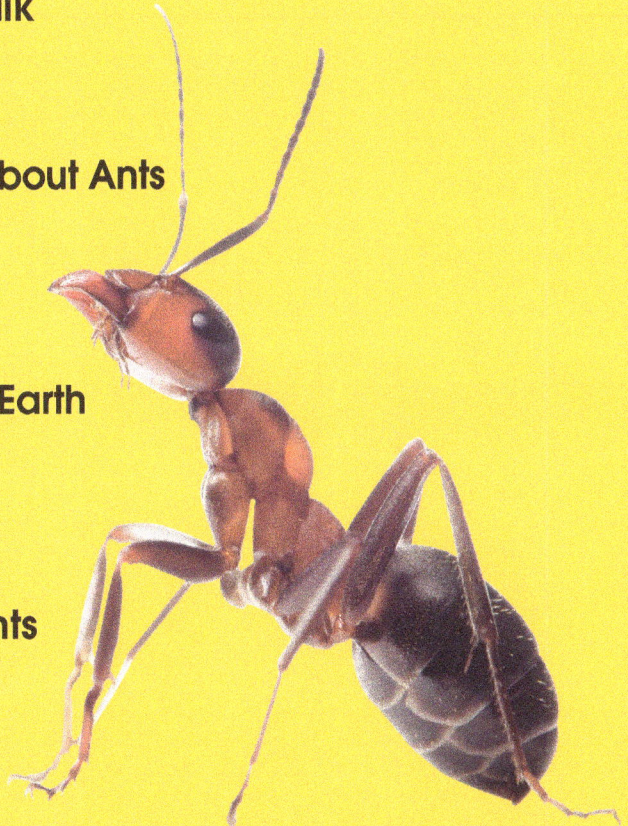

# What Are Ants?

Ants are **insects**. They are related to wasps and bees.

**KEY WORD**

**Insects:** small animals with six legs. Their bodies are covered by a hard shell.

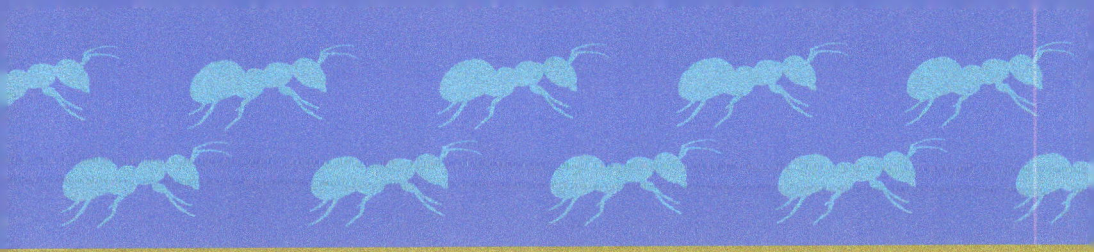

A group of ants is called an army or a colony. They are very helpful to people, other animals, and Earth.

## A Closer Look

Ants are between 0.03 and 2 inches (0.08 and 5.2 centimeters) long. Only some ants have wings.

Ants have small waists. Scientists can tell different types of ants apart by counting the number of spaces in their waist.

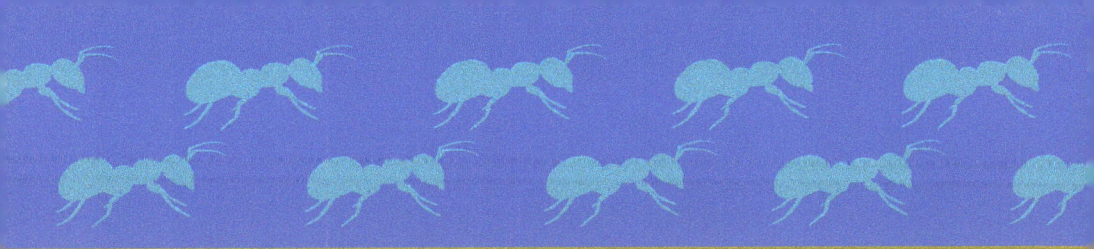

Ants have feelers on their head called antennae. Antennae help ants recognize other ants.

Ants have strong jaws. They use their jaws for biting, cutting, and carrying.

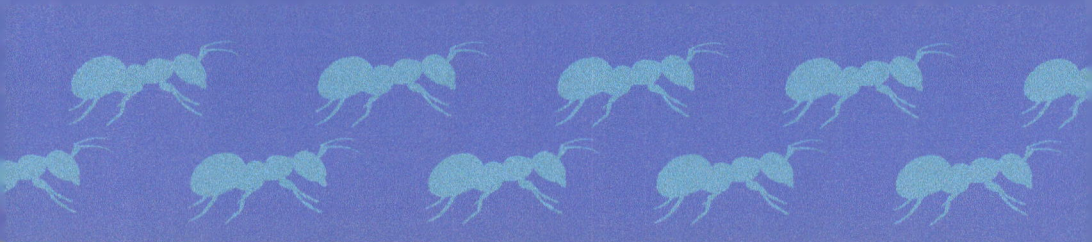

## Where Do Ants Live?

Most ants build nests underground. Every colony has a queen. Queen ants lay eggs. Worker ants find food, care for the queen's eggs, and protect their home.

Ants live all over the world. Jack jumper ants live in Australia. Bullet ants are found in the Amazon rainforest. Black carpenter ants live east of the Rocky Mountains.

Arctic Ocean

Rocky Mountains

Europe

Australia

North America

Atlantic Ocean

Africa

South America

Amazon rainforest

Pacific Ocean

Southern Ocean

0 — 2,000 miles

N

0 — 4,000 kilometers

**Legend**
▢ Land
▢ Ocean

Antarctica

9

## What Do Ants Eat?

Ants eat many different foods. Many ants eat grass, seeds, and berries. Others eat a sweet liquid made by tiny bugs called aphids. Some kinds of ants eat other insects.

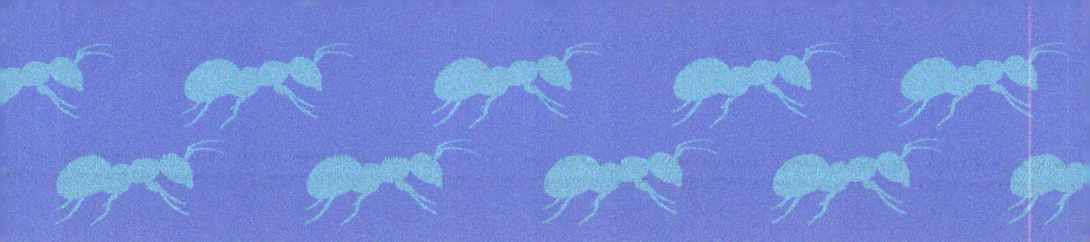

Leafcutter ants grow **fungi** gardens in their nests. They bring pieces of leaves to their nests to feed the fungi. The ants then eat the fungi they have grown.

**KEY WORD**

**Fungi:** living beings that are not plants or animals. Mushrooms and mold are both fungi.

11

# How Do Ants Talk to Each Other?

Ants leave chemicals around their **habitats**. The smell of these chemicals can warn other ants of danger or tell them where to find food.

**KEY WORD**

**Habitats:** the places a plant or animal lives. Different animals need different habitats.

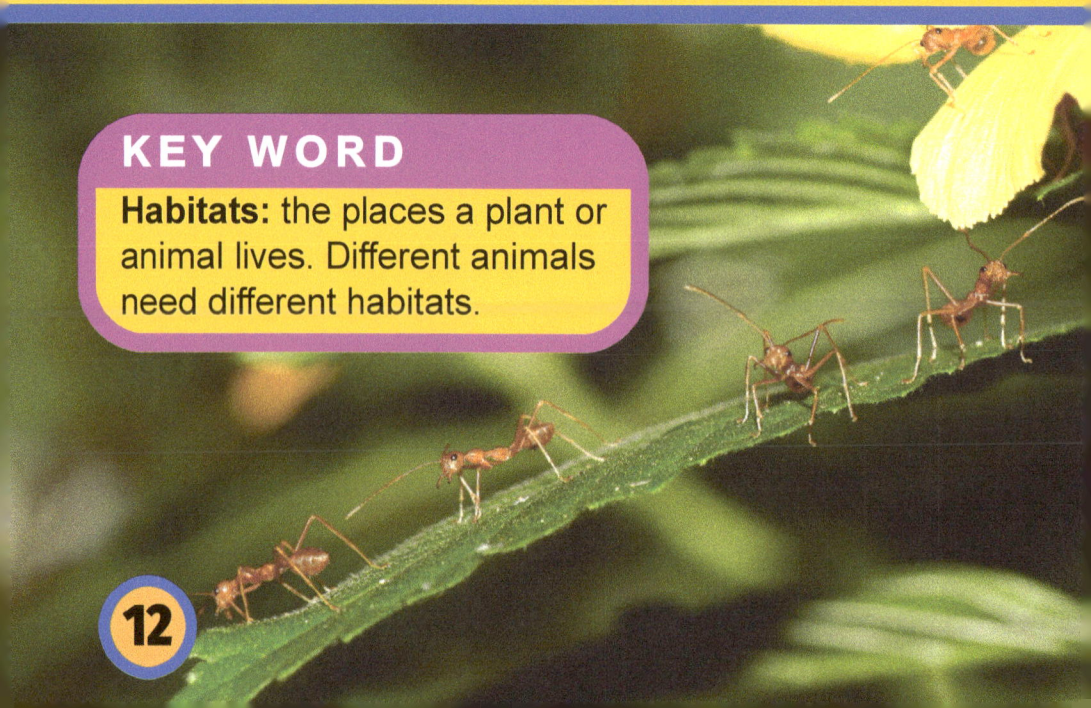

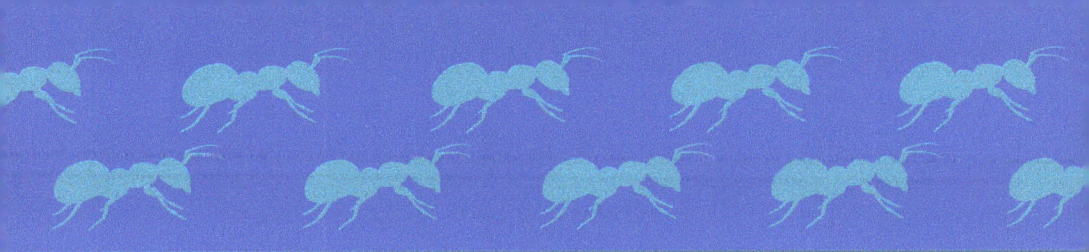

Ants use their antennae to smell these chemicals. They also use their antennae to gently touch each other. Every touch has a different meaning.

Some ants will touch each other on the head. This means they want the other ant to share their food.

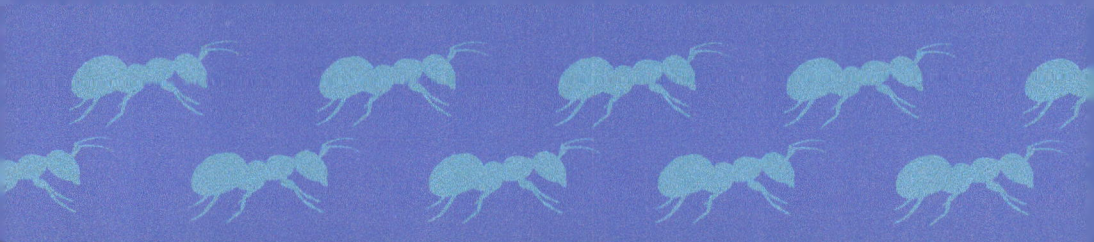

# Ant Life Cycle

The queen is the only ant in a nest who lays eggs. She will lay thousands of eggs in her lifetime.

Ant eggs hatch into larvae. Ant larvae are small, white and legless. They are looked after by worker ants.

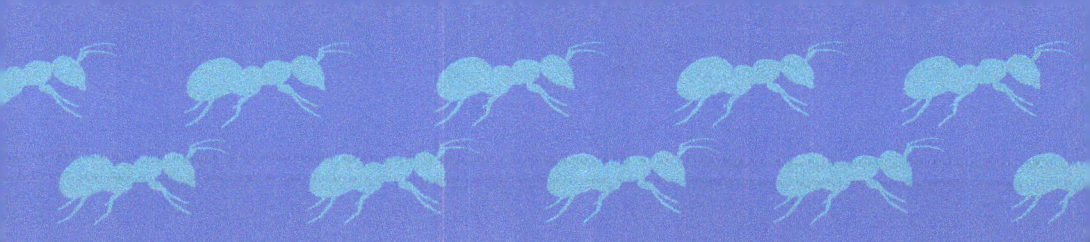

Ant larvae create hard shells around themselves called cocoons. Young ants in cocoons are called pupae. They stay in their cocoons for a few weeks.

Ants leave their cocoons as adults. Most worker ants only live for 6 to 10 weeks. Queens can live for up to 15 years.

# Curious Facts About Ants

Ants can carry objects that weigh 50 times their bodyweight.

Some ant nests can be thousands of miles long. These are called supercolonies.

Ants do not have ears. Some do not have eyes.

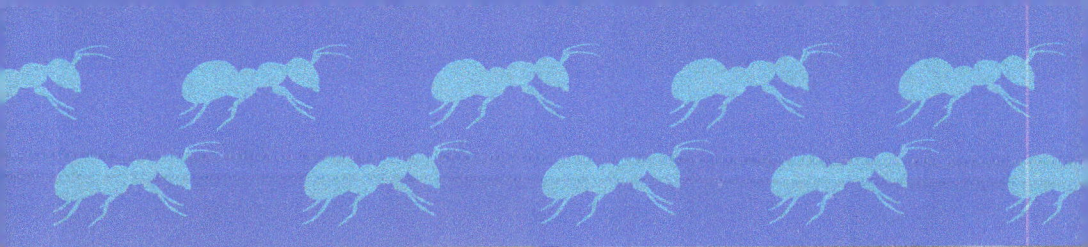

Ants have been on Earth for at least 50 million years.

Ants breathe through tiny holes in their bodies. They do not have lungs.

Some ants create traps to catch live food.

17

## Kinds of Ants

There are more than 10,000 kinds of ants. They are all different shapes and sizes. They can be black, red, brown, or yellow.

Carpenter ants can be black or red. They build their nests by making tunnels in wood.

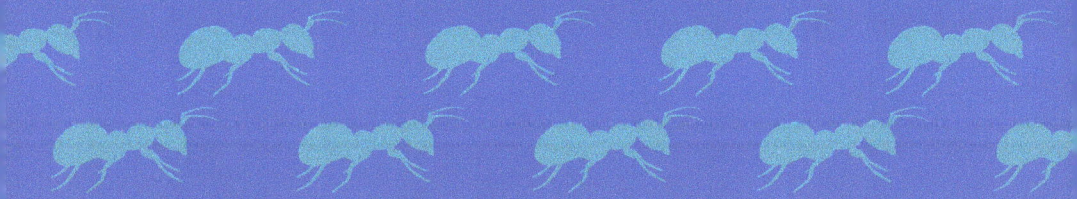

Honeypot ants store food in their bellies. Some get so big they cannot move.

Fire ants are very protective of their nests. They have sharp stingers that spray poison when they sting.

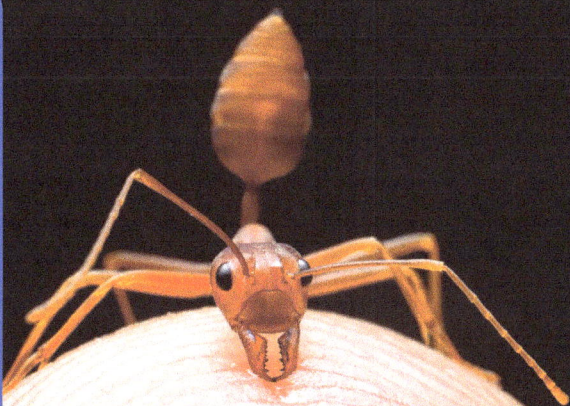

19

## How Ants Help Other Animals

Some caterpillars look like ant larvae. One kind of red ant will bring these caterpillars into their nests to care for them.

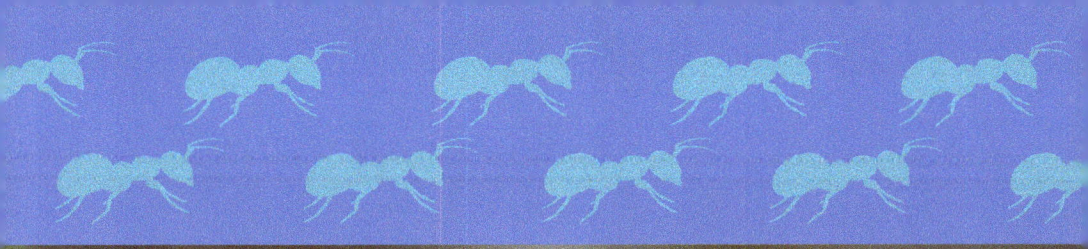

The ants feed
the caterpillars.
They also protect
the caterpillars
from **predators**
until they are
ready to turn
into butterflies.

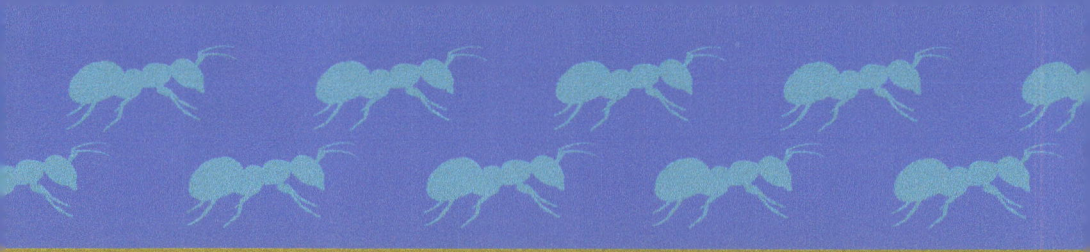

## How Ants Help Earth

Ants dig many tunnels. Digging turns the soil and adds air to it. This allows water to more easily reach plant roots to help them grow.

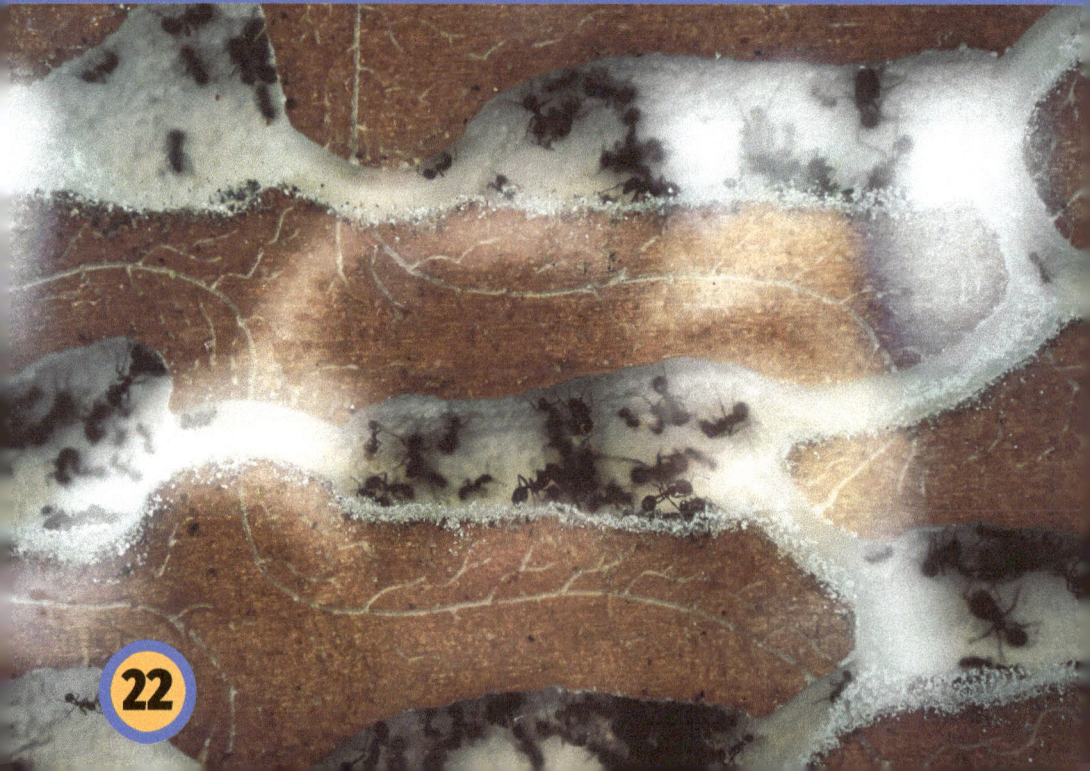

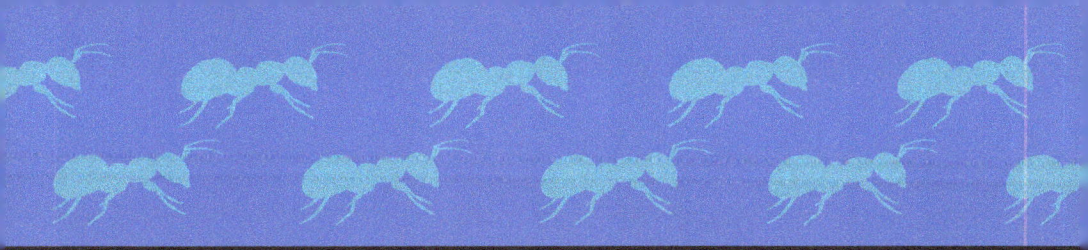

Ants help plants grow in new places. They bring lots of plant seeds into their underground tunnels. Some of these seeds grow into new plants.

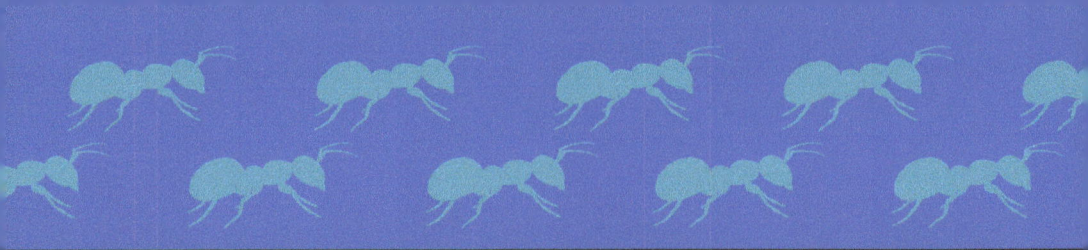

## How Ants Help Humans

Ants are great at working together and problem solving. Scientists are studying this behaviour. They have created computer systems that copy ant behaviour.

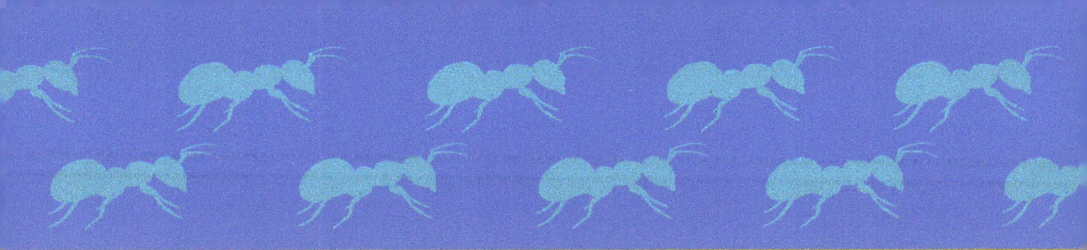

These computer systems are helping mail carriers find the fastest path from one house to another. Finding a faster path can also help ambulances reach people more quickly.

## Ants in Danger

Some ants are endangered. This means there are very few of them left. The red-barbed ant is one of the hardest animals to find in Britain. Other ants have taken over their habitat.

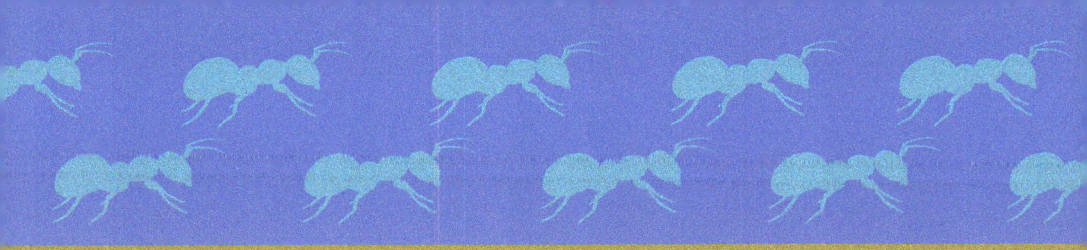

The dinosaur ant is one of the oldest kinds of ants. They are only found in Australia. Forest fires have destroyed much of their habitat.

27

## How To Help Ants

Ants can easily find their way into people's homes. Some people use chemicals to get rid of them. These chemicals often kill the ants.

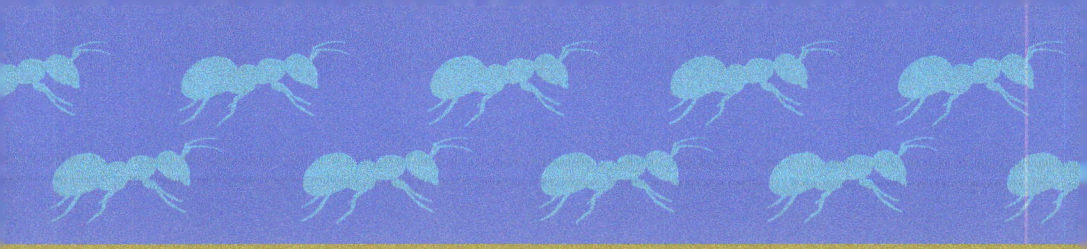

Many people are using strong smells to keep ants away. Ants do not like the smell of mint, lemon juice, or cinnamon. People place these items around their house or picnic area to keep ants away.

# Quiz

Test your knowledge of ants by answering the following questions. The questions are based on what you have read in this book. The answers are listed on the bottom of the next page.

**1** What is a group of ants called?

**2** Where do most ants build their nests?

**3** What do ants use their antennae for?

**4** Who is the only ant in a nest that can lay eggs?

**5** How do ants breathe?

**6** What are predators?

# Explore other books in the Animals That Make a Difference series.

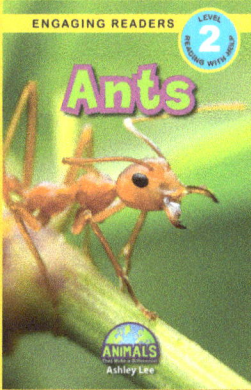
ENGAGING READERS — LEVEL 2
Ants
ANIMALS
Ashley Lee

ENGAGING READERS — LEVEL 2
Beavers
ANIMALS
Ashley Lee

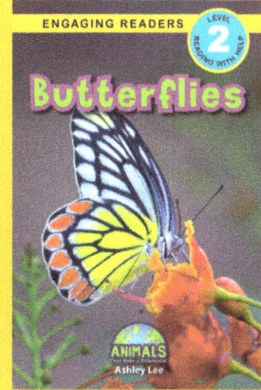
ENGAGING READERS — LEVEL 2
Butterflies
ANIMALS
Ashley Lee

ENGAGING READERS — LEVEL 2
Dogs
ANIMALS
Ashley Lee

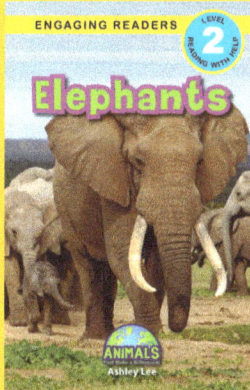
ENGAGING READERS — LEVEL 2
Elephants
ANIMALS
Ashley Lee

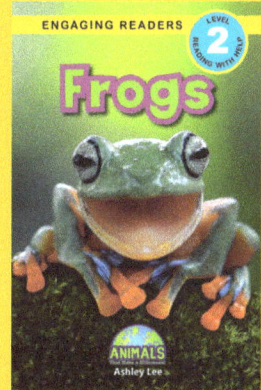
ENGAGING READERS — LEVEL 2
Frogs
ANIMALS
Ashley Lee

ENGAGING READERS — LEVEL 2
Llamas
ANIMALS
Ashley Lee &
Jared Siemens

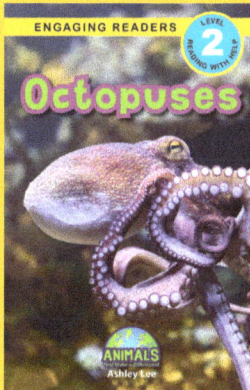
ENGAGING READERS — LEVEL 2
Octopuses
ANIMALS
Ashley Lee

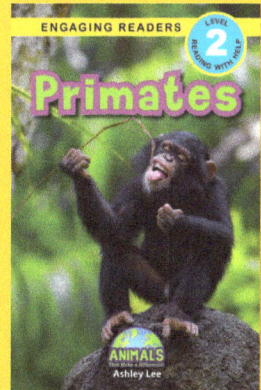
ENGAGING READERS — LEVEL 2
Primates
ANIMALS
Ashley Lee

Visit www.engagebooks.com to explore more Engaging Readers.

**Answers:** 1. An army or colony 2. Underground 3. To smell chemicals and touch each other 4. The queen 5. Through tiny holes in their bodies 6. Animals that hunt other animals for food